This Book Belongs To:

_____

Congratulations!

This book is dedicated to **YOU** for taking this important step to improving your penmanship!

This Handwriting Workbook is designed to help teens and adults build skills in penmanship in order to write clearly and neatly.

You will have plenty of repetitive practice and the funny and sarcastic quotes will motivate you to keep practicing!

TABLE OF CONTENTS

If you enjoy this book, we would really appreciate it if you could please leave a review on Amazon! Your kind words will inspire us to make more like it!

5 5 5 5 5 5 5 5 5 5 5 5 5 5 5 5 5 5

6 6 6 6 6 6 6 6 6 6 6 6 6 6 6 6 6 6

7 7 7 7 7 7 7 7 7 7 7 7 7 7 7 7 7 7

8 8 8 8 8 8 8 8 8 8 8 8 8 8 8 8 8

9 9 9 9 9 9 9 9 9 9 9 9 9 9 9 9 9 9

one one one one one one one one one

two two two two two two two two two

three three three three three three three three three

four four four four four four four four

five five five five five five five five five

six six six six six six six six six six

seven seven seven seven seven seven seven

eight eight eight eight eight eight eight

nine nine nine nine nine nine nine nine

ten ten ten ten ten ten ten ten ten ten

eleven eleven eleven eleven eleven eleven

twelve twelve twelve twelve twelve twelve

thirteen thirteen thirteen thirteen thirteen

fourteen fourteen fourteen fourteen fourteen

fifteen fifteen fifteen fifteen fifteen fifteen

sixteen sixteen sixteen sixteen sixteen

seventeen seventeen seventeen seventeen

eighteen eighteen eighteen eighteen eighteen

nineteen nineteen nineteen nineteen nineteen

twenty twenty twenty twenty twenty

thirty thirty thirty thirty thirty thirty

forty forty forty forty forty forty forty

fifty fifty fifty fifty fifty fifty fifty fifty

sixty sixty sixty sixty sixty sixty sixty

seventy seventy seventy seventy seventy

eighty eighty eighty eighty eighty eighty

ninety ninety ninety ninety ninety

hundred hundred hundred hundred hundred

thousand thousand thousand thousand

apple apple apple apple apple apple apple

banana banana banana banana banana

cartoon cartoon cartoon cartoon cartoon

dragon dragon dragon dragon dragon

elephant elephant elephant elephant

friction friction friction friction friction friction

giant giant giant giant giant giant giant

hiccup hiccup hiccup hiccup hiccup hiccup

indigo indigo indigo indigo indigo indigo

joking joking joking joking joking joking

knight knight knight knight knight knight

likely likely likely likely likely likely

melody melody melody melody melody

notebook notebook notebook notebook

offend offend offend offend offend offend

pecan pecan pecan pecan pecan pecan

quick quick quick quick quick quick quick

rebel rebel rebel rebel rebel rebel rebel

satire satire satire satire satire satire satire

trick trick trick trick trick trick trick trick

universe universe universe universe universe

vacant vacant vacant vacant vacant

waist waist waist waist waist waist waist

xerox xerox xerox xerox xerox xerox xerox

yawn yawn yawn yawn yawn yawn

zany zany zany zany zany zany zany

To get rid of unwanted junk during the holidays... Put it in an Amazon box and leave it on the front porch.

To get rid of unwanted junk during the holidays... Put it in an Amazon box and leave it on the front porch.

To get rid of unwanted junk during the holidays... Put it in an Amazon box and leave it on the front porch.

I always read my wife's horoscope to see
what kind of day I'm going to have.
I always read my wife's horoscope to see
what kind of day I'm going to have.
I always read my wife's horoscope to see
what kind of day I'm going to have.

I'm bored. I think I'll go to the mall, find a really great parking spot and sit in my car with the reverse lights on.

I'm bored. I think I'll go to the mall, find a really great parking spot and sit in my car with the reverse lights on.

I'm bored. I think I'll go to the mall, find a really great parking spot and sit in my car with the reverse lights on.

If you're sitting in public and a stranger sits next to you, just stare straight ahead and say, "Did you bring the money?"

If you're sitting in public and a stranger sits next to you, just stare straight ahead and say, "Did you bring the money?"

If you're sitting in public and a stranger sits next to you, just stare straight ahead and say, "Did you bring the money?"

When you ask me what I am doing today,
and I say "nothing," it does not mean I am
free. It means I am doing nothing.
When you ask me what I am doing today,
and I say "nothing," it does not mean I am
free. It means I am doing nothing.
When you ask me what I am doing today,
and I say "nothing," it does not mean I am
free. It means I am doing nothing.

Remember, if you lose a sock in the dryer, it comes back as a Tupperware lid that doesn't fit any of your containers.

Remember, if you lose a sock in the dryer, it comes back as a Tupperware lid that doesn't fit any of your containers.

Remember, if you lose a sock in the dryer, it comes back as a Tupperware lid that doesn't fit any of your containers.

Sixty might be the new forty, but nine
o'clock is the new midnight.
Sixty might be the new forty, but nine
o'clock is the new midnight.
Sixty might be the new forty, but nine
o'clock is the new midnight.

When one door closes and another opens, you
are probably in prison.
When one door closes and another opens, you
are probably in prison.
When one door closes and another opens, you
are probably in prison.

When I say "the other day," I could be referring to any time between yesterday and fifteen years ago.

When I say "the other day," I could be referring to any time between yesterday and fifteen years ago.

When I say "the other day," I could be referring to any time between yesterday and fifteen years ago.

I don't mean to interrupt people, I just randomly remember things and get really excited.

I don't mean to interrupt people, I just randomly remember things and get really excited.

I don't mean to interrupt people, I just randomly remember things and get really excited.

I had my patience tested. Turns out I'm
negative.
I had my patience tested. Turns out I'm
negative.
I had my patience tested. Turns out I'm
negative.

If you answer the phone with "Hello, you're
on the air!" most telemarketers will quickly
hang up...
If you answer the phone with "Hello, you're
on the air!" most telemarketers will quickly
hang up...
If you answer the phone with "Hello, you're
on the air!" most telemarketers will quickly
hang up...

That moment when you walk into a spider
web and suddenly turn into a karate master.
That moment when you walk into a spider
web and suddenly turn into a karate master.
That moment when you walk into a spider
web and suddenly turn into a karate master.

When I ask for directions, please don't use
words like "East."

When I ask for directions, please don't use
words like "East."

When I ask for directions, please don't use
words like "East."

The older I get, the earlier it gets late.

The older I get, the earlier it gets late.

The older I get, the earlier it gets late.

Sweating while you shop counts as exercise.

Sweating while you shop counts as exercise.

Sweating while you shop counts as exercise.

I remember being able to get up without
making sound effects... Good times.
I remember being able to get up without
making sound effects... Good times.
I remember being able to get up without
making sound effects... Good times.

My luck is like a bald guy winning a comb.

My luck is like a bald guy winning a comb.

My luck is like a bald guy winning a comb.

My favorite party trick is not going.

My favorite party trick is not going.

My favorite party trick is not going.

Don't bother walking a mile in my shoes,
that would be boring. Spend thirty seconds
in my head, that'll freak you right out.
Don't bother walking a mile in my shoes,
that would be boring. Spend thirty seconds
in my head, that'll freak you right out.
Don't bother walking a mile in my shoes,
that would be boring. Spend thirty seconds
in my head, that'll freak you right out.

Cop: "Please step out of the car." Me: I'm too

drunk, you get in."

Cop: "Please step out of the car." Me: I'm too

drunk, you get in."

Cop: "Please step out of the car." Me: I'm too

drunk, you get in."

Sometimes someone unexpected comes into your life outta nowhere, makes your heart race and changes you forever... We call these people cops.

Sometimes someone unexpected comes into your life outta nowhere, makes your heart race and changes you forever... We call these people cops.

Sometimes someone unexpected comes into your life outta nowhere, makes your heart race and changes you forever... We call these people cops.

I can always tell when you are lying. Your lips are moving.

I can always tell when you are lying. Your lips are moving.

I can always tell when you are lying. Your lips are moving.

When people see you lying down with your eyes closed, they still ask "Are You Sleeping?" "No, I'm training to die."

When people see you lying down with your eyes closed, they still ask "Are You Sleeping?" "No, I'm training to die."

When people see you lying down with your eyes closed, they still ask "Are You Sleeping?" "No, I'm training to die."

The trash gets picked up tomorrow. Be ready.

The trash gets picked up tomorrow. Be ready.

The trash gets picked up tomorrow. Be ready.

Underestimate me. That will be fun.

Underestimate me. That will be fun.

Underestimate me. That will be fun.

Sleeping is my drug, my bed is my dealer
and my alarm clock is the police.
Sleeping is my drug, my bed is my dealer
and my alarm clock is the police.
Sleeping is my drug, my bed is my dealer
and my alarm clock is the police.

You look good when your eyes are closed, but
you look the best when my eyes are closed.
You look good when your eyes are closed, but
you look the best when my eyes are closed.
You look good when your eyes are closed, but
you look the best when my eyes are closed.

Life is hard; it's harder if you're stupid.

Life is hard; it's harder if you're stupid.

Life is hard; it's harder if you're stupid.

I'll get over it. I just need to be dramatic first.

I'll get over it. I just need to be dramatic first.

I'll get over it. I just need to be dramatic first.

People say nothing is impossible, but I do
nothing every day.
People say nothing is impossible, but I do
nothing every day.
People say nothing is impossible, but I do
nothing every day.

The four most beautiful words in our common language: I told you so.

The four most beautiful words in our common language: I told you so.

The four most beautiful words in our common language: I told you so.

If you want to change the world, do it while
you're single. Once you're married you can't
even change the channel.
If you want to change the world, do it while
you're single. Once you're married you can't
even change the channel.
If you want to change the world, do it while
you're single. Once you're married you can't
even change the channel.

What do people do with all the extra time
they save by writing 'ok' instead of 'okay'?
What do people do with all the extra time
they save by writing 'ok' instead of 'okay'?
What do people do with all the extra time
they save by writing 'ok' instead of 'okay'?

There's no better vacation than my boss being on vacation.

There's no better vacation than my boss being on vacation.

There's no better vacation than my boss being on vacation.

I don't always tolerate stupid people. But when I do, I'm probably at work.

I don't always tolerate stupid people. But when I do, I'm probably at work.

I don't always tolerate stupid people. But when I do, I'm probably at work.

Don't mistake my efficiency as meaning I want to do your job, too.

Don't mistake my efficiency as meaning I want to do your job, too.

Don't mistake my efficiency as meaning I want to do your job, too.

If you find me offensive, then I suggest you quit finding me.

If you find me offensive, then I suggest you quit finding me.

If you find me offensive, then I suggest you quit finding me.

If I had nine of my fingers missing I wouldn't type any slower.

If I had nine of my fingers missing I wouldn't type any slower.

If I had nine of my fingers missing I wouldn't type any slower.

I'm sorry I hurt your feelings when I called you stupid. I really thought you already knew.

I'm sorry I hurt your feelings when I called you stupid. I really thought you already knew.

I'm sorry I hurt your feelings when I called you stupid. I really thought you already knew.

When one door closes, another opens. Or you can open the closed door. That's how doors work.

When one door closes, another opens. Or you can open the closed door. That's how doors work.

When one door closes, another opens. Or you can open the closed door. That's how doors work.

Sometimes I need what only you can
provide: your absence.
Sometimes I need what only you can
provide: your absence.
Sometimes I need what only you can
provide: your absence.

An apple a day keeps anything away if you throw it hard enough.

An apple a day keeps anything away if you throw it hard enough.

An apple a day keeps anything away if you throw it hard enough.

Tell me, is being stupid your profession, or are you just gifted?

Tell me, is being stupid your profession, or are you just gifted?

Tell me, is being stupid your profession, or are you just gifted?

Silence is golden. Duct tape is silver.

Silence is golden. Duct tape is silver.

Silence is golden. Duct tape is silver.

Ugliness can be fixed, stupidity is forever.

Ugliness can be fixed, stupidity is forever.

Ugliness can be fixed, stupidity is forever.

I'm kinda busy right now, can I ignore you some other time?

I'm kinda busy right now, can I ignore you some other time?

I'm kinda busy right now, can I ignore you some other time?

Find your patience before I lose mine.

Find your patience before I lose mine.

Find your patience before I lose mine.

Life's good, you should get one.

Life's good, you should get one.

Life's good, you should get one.

If had a dollar for every smart thing you
say, I'd be poor.
If had a dollar for every smart thing you
say, I'd be poor.
If had a dollar for every smart thing you
say, I'd be poor.

I'm sorry, while you were talking, I was trying to figure out where the hell you got the idea I cared.

I'm sorry, while you were talking, I was trying to figure out where the hell you got the idea I cared.

I'm sorry, while you were talking, I was trying to figure out where the hell you got the idea I cared.

Sarcasm is the secret language that everyone
uses when they want to say something mean
to your face.

Sarcasm is the secret language that everyone
uses when they want to say something mean
to your face.

Sarcasm is the secret language that everyone
uses when they want to say something mean
to your face.

If at first, you don't succeed, skydiving is not for you.

If at first, you don't succeed, skydiving is not for you.

If at first, you don't succeed, skydiving is not for you.

People say that laughter is the best medicine...
your face must be curing the world.
People say that laughter is the best medicine...
your face must be curing the world.
People say that laughter is the best medicine...
your face must be curing the world.

I never forget a face, but in your case, I'll be glad to make an exception.
I never forget a face, but in your case, I'll be glad to make an exception.
I never forget a face, but in your case, I'll be glad to make an exception.

If you think nobody cares if you're alive,

try missing a couple of car payments.

If you think nobody cares if you're alive,

try missing a couple of car payments.

If you think nobody cares if you're alive,

try missing a couple of car payments.

My neighbor's diary says that I have boundary issues.

My neighbor's diary says that I have boundary issues.

My neighbor's diary says that I have boundary issues.

I would like to apologize to anyone I have not offended yet. Please be patient. I will get to you shortly.

I would like to apologize to anyone I have not offended yet. Please be patient. I will get to you shortly.

I would like to apologize to anyone I have not offended yet. Please be patient. I will get to you shortly.

Sometimes the amount of self-control it takes to not say what's on my mind is so immense, I need a nap afterward.

Sometimes the amount of self-control it takes to not say what's on my mind is so immense, I need a nap afterward.

Sometimes the amount of self-control it takes to not say what's on my mind is so immense, I need a nap afterward.

The stuff you heard about me is a lie. I'm
way worse.
The stuff you heard about me is a lie. I'm
way worse.
The stuff you heard about me is a lie. I'm
way worse.

Made in United States
Troutdale, OR
11/15/2024

24838390R00051